ICEBERG ALLEY

By MADELYN KLEIN ANDERSON

ICEBERG ALLEY

Illustrated with
photographs and maps

Julian Messner
New York

Published by Julian Messner, a Division of Simon & Schuster, Inc.
a Gulf + Western Company
1 West 39 Street, New York, N.Y. 10018. All rights reserved.

Copyright © 1976 by Madelyn Klein Anderson

Printed in the United States of America
Design by Marjorie Zaum

Library of Congress Cataloging in Publication Data

Anderson, Madelyn Klein.
    Iceberg Alley.

    Includes index.
    SUMMARY: Discusses the formation, characteristics, and movements
of icebergs, their danger to ships, and the work of the ice patrol who
cover "Iceberg Alley" in the North Atlantic, searching for the huge blocks
of ice and warning ocean traffic.
    1. Icebergs — Juvenile literature. 2. International ice patrol —
Juvenile literature. 3. United States. Coast Guard — Juvenile literature.
[1. Icebergs. 2. International ice patrol. 3. United States.
Coast Guard] I. Title.
VK1299.A52   363.2   76-28234
ISBN 0-671-32804-2

To Justin

ACKNOWLEDGMENTS

The author wishes to express the deepest gratitude to the many members of the United States Coast Guard who gave of their time, their knowledge, and themselves:

PAC Paul C. Scotti, who was involved from beginning to end, and whose concern was far more than duty.

CDR Albert "Don" Super, who gave so much of his valuable time and knowledge; LTJGs Kenneth Knutson and Thomas Neill for their erudition; James E. More and Jeff Evers and all the other men of the International Ice Patrol; and PA1 Joseph D. Amato for the photos he took on the flight through Iceberg Alley.

And to Roland Buster, Tom Pigage, John Odom, Daniel Daneker, Edward Allen, Michael Bunker, Ron Seale, Butch Hampton, and Gary McElroy—last but not least—who honored me by making me a part of the crew of CG1341: you are very much a part of this book, and more.

The author also wishes to thank the editor, Lee M. Hoffman, and copyeditor, William Jaber, for their assistance.

DEPARTMENT OF TRANSPORTATION
UNITED STATES COAST GUARD MAILING ADDRESS:
Commander
International Ice Patrol
Governors Island
New York, NY 10004

2 August 1976

        The missions of the U.S. Coast Guard are many and varied. Most
are concerned with the humanitarian task of safety of life at sea.   In
keeping with this purpose, the International Ice Patrol, headquartered
at the Coast Guard Support Center, Governors Island, N.Y., guards the
dangerous Grand Banks of Newfoundland against the iceberg threat to the
North Atlantic mariner.
        Since 1914 the Coast Guard has managed and operated the Internation-
al Ice Patrol service. This service involves the observations and study
of ice and ocean conditions in the vicinity of the Grand Banks and the
dissemination of this ice information to shipping. Established shortly
after the sinking of the liner TITANIC, one of the greatest sea tragedies
of all time, the Ice Patrol is sponsored and funded jointly by the nations
whose ships sail these heavily traveled shipping routes through the world's
most formidable waters. Thus, the Ice Patrol is truely an outstanding
example of international cooperation toward the common goal of greater
maritime safety. In more than six decades of Ice Patrol vigilance against
the iceberg threat, not a single ship or life has been lost due to a ship
collision with ice outside the Ice Patrol's warned limits of danger.
        With honor and gratitude the Coast Guardsmen of the International
Ice Patrol thank Ms. Anderson for bringing to you the story of this long
standing, successful service.

                                        A. D. SUPER
                                        Commander, U.S. Coast Guard
                                        Officer-In-Charge
                                        International Ice Patrol

CONTENTS

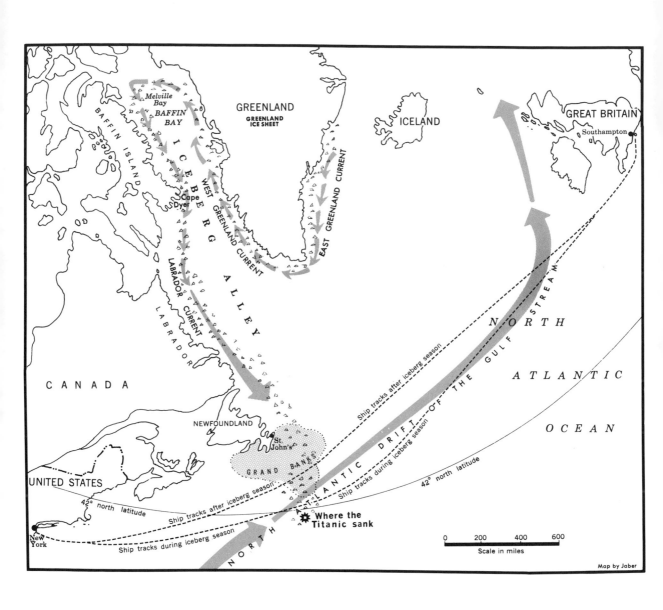

1

THREE SHARP BLOWS ON A GONG...

GLOWING WITH LIGHTS, THE SHIP MOVED SWIFTLY through the black, still water. Smoke streamed from three of her four great funnels, clouding over the brilliant stars.

Proud, sure of herself, she was the largest ship in the world, the British **RMS Titanic**. It was April 14, 1912, and she was passing over the Grand Banks area of the North Atlantic Ocean, about 800 miles from New York. She was near the end of her maiden (first) voyage.

The night grew suddenly colder. Shivering, some passengers turned up the electric stoves as they prepared for bed. Others, not wanting to end the pleasant evening, turned to the warmth of elegant smoking rooms and card rooms, and conversation.

On the bridge, two officers also chatted briefly. One was going off duty, the other coming on. Both kept their eyes on the sea ahead as they spoke. Captain Smith had ordered a sharp watch kept for icebergs. There had been many warnings from passing ships of ice in the area.

The *Titanic* starts on her ill-fated voyage. She was advertised as the most luxurious and safest ship in the world. Many famous people were aboard.

Lights were put out forward of the bridge in order to see into the darkness better. Two lookouts were sent to the crow's nest, a wire cage on a mast, 95 feet above the water. It would have helped if they had binoculars, but there were none.

It would have helped, too, if the sea were not so calm. Then the men could see the water breaking around the base of an iceberg — even if they could not see the berg itself.

But the officers were not especially concerned. Their ship was the greatest afloat. The night was clear. Of course, if the weather changed, they would slow down, as Captain Smith had ordered. But they saw no need to slow the ship now. Not that they were trying to break any speed records for the crossing. The engines were new and had to be broken in before they could be run at top speed.

10

They didn't know that the radio operator had received a warning of an iceberg directly in their path. But he had been too busy sending messages for passengers to families and friends in New York to deliver it to the bridge. And there had been so many messages about ice already. . . .

The officers parted. Sea and sky remained clear, and the ship moved swiftly on its course.

Then — three sharp blows on the lookouts' gong shattered the silence. Danger ahead!

Over the speaking tube came the shout, "Iceberg dead ahead!" It was less than 500 yards away. The duty officer signalled a hard starboard (right) turn and a reverse engines. The helmsman steered right — and into the berg.

The iceberg scraped along the starboard side of the ship for almost half its length, leaving behind some shavings of ice. A few hardy passengers enjoyed playing with them.

Some of the card players stopped for a minute to watch the iceberg sail by the portholes. Then they returned to their game. There seemed no reason for worry.

A passenger later said that if he had been holding a glass filled to the brim with water, not a drop would have spilled. There had been barely a bump or a quiver. There was only the sudden quiet, as the engines stopped. The passengers joked that Captain Smith, a fussy man, had stopped to paint a scratch that the iceberg had made.

But the iceberg had made more than a scratch. In 10

seconds, less than the time it takes you to read this sentence, an underwater ledge of the iceberg had sliced open the great ship like a can opener.

The ship was slowly sinking — and there weren't enough lifeboats. The laws of that time did not require lifeboat spaces for every person on board a ship. Women and children were sent into the lifeboats first. And many boats went over the side half empty, because men were not allowed on.

To prevent panic, the engineers kept the generators going so the lights stayed on, and the band played lively ragtime tunes.

They were playing "Autumn" when the **Titanic** finally nosed over, $2\frac{1}{2}$ hours after the collision. People jumped or were thrown into the water as the ship's stern (rear) pointed almost straight up in the air. Her lights went out, and she slid under the water with barely a ripple.

Those in the lifeboats watched in horror. Fearful that their boats might swamp, they picked up only a few of the people struggling in the icy water. Soon the water was quiet — some 1500 people had died. The exact number is still unknown.

A few hours later, the passenger ship **Carpathia** rescued the 711 survivors. With amazing skill, she had dodged icebergs at high speed all night, to reach the lifeboats at dawn. The rising sun glowed pink on a field of ice and a number of icebergs, large and small, moving toward the boats. No one had seen them during the night. Which was

Photograph taken from the rescue ship *Carpathia* of *Titanic* survivors in lifeboats.

the berg that had sunk the **Titanic**? Was it any of them? It was impossible to tell.

For the iceberg that sank the largest ship in the world showed no scars from the encounter. It simply moved on, to where the currents and winds took it. It had already been traveling for two or three years through the waters of Iceberg Alley. It had entered the North Atlantic only a week or so before, and reached the same place in that ocean at the same time as the **Titanic**. Then it moved into the Gulf Stream, where it met the only force in the world strong enough to destroy it — heat.

The iceberg melted and joined the waters of the Gulf Stream. Moisture evaporating from these waters rose to the sky, to be stored in clouds. Some of the moisture fell again, as snow over Greenland to the north — the weather factory for the North Atlantic. This snow joined the great sheet of ice covering that huge island. And perhaps 500 or 1,000 years from now, part of that ice will break off and become another iceberg traveling down Iceberg Alley.

2

RIVERS OF ICE

ICEBERGS HAVE THEIR BEGINNINGS IN THE SNOWS that fall above the snowline. The **snowline** is the altitude, or height, above which there is always snow on the ground. The snowline is at sea level, as in the Antarctic. Or the snowline is higher as temperatures grow higher. There is a snowline even at the Equator, at the top of very high mountains.

Above the snowline, the snow never completely melts, even in summer. Most of it remains, to be covered by the next winter's snow. The weight of this snow cover rounds off the pointed edges of the feathery snow crystals underneath. The rounded crystals join together into **firn**, or last year's snow. Another year, another snow layer, and the old firn underneath is turned into ice.

Layer after layer presses down, squeezing out most of the air between the ice crystals, compressing them into a dense, solid mineral, like rock.

Hundreds or thousands of years of these heavy layers

of ice accumulate. Under their great weight or pressure, the solid rock-like ice at the bottom moves.

Slowly, slowly, so slowly it cannot be seen, these lower layers of ice move, carrying the upper layers with them.

These moving bodies of land ice are **glaciers** (**glay**-shers).

As the glaciers move and turn corners, great cracks called **crevasses** (kruh-**vasses**) open in the ice. And as they move, they sweep up everything under, around and before them. This is **drift** — earth, rocks, boulders — and it grinds and gouges, scrapes and scours the land as it is carried along. Where the glaciers melt a little, some of the drift drops out, and is left behind along the edges or on the bottom of the glacier. These droppings are called **moraine** (more-**ain**). There are ridges and piles and sheets of moraine all over the world where glaciers once moved. Plymouth Rock is a bit of glacial moraine.

Glaciologists, scientists who study glaciers, have divided them into many different kinds. But there are two main kinds: mountain glaciers and ice sheets.

Mountain glaciers start on high mountain snowfields and move through valleys between the mountains. Pulled by gravity, and pushed by their own pressure, they always move downward. They are kept active by snow avalanching on them. These are the glaciers mountain climbers know of, the glaciers of ranges like the Alps, the Himalayas, the Rockies.

16

A glacier in West Greenland,
with many crevasses.

The arrows point to lateral
moraine.

Mountain glaciers often end in lakes or bays. The glacier may have made the lake, by dropping moraine in a valley, damming it up. Then glacial melt water fills the basin.

Sometimes mountain glaciers end on a high flat plain. They spread out, forming a lake of ice called a **piedmont** (**peed**-mont) glacier. Some glaciologists think that piedmont glaciers grew so high near the North and South Poles that they covered the mountains they started from — and became the ice sheets of Greenland and Antarctica.

Ice sheets are glaciers which move out in all directions from a central source on a high plateau, or flat area. They can even move uphill, pushed by the great pressure within them. Snow pours on their center, like batter poured from a pitcher — and the ice sheets move out just like pancakes on a griddle. And, like pancakes, the outer edges of ice sheets are thinner than their center.

During the Ice Ages, ice sheets were so large and deep that they moved over entire continents. They were, in fact, called **continental glaciers**. They moved over half the world. Then climates became warmer, less snow fell, and the continental glaciers grew thinner. The pressure within them lessened. The glaciers could not move out fast enough to replace the melting ice at their edges, and so they became smaller — and smaller. They stopped their retreat only when they reached the coldest parts of the earth, the polar regions.

Today, only the Antarctic ice sheet can be called a

continental glacier. It covers the entire Antarctic continent. Scientists at the Pole Station have measured it at about 9,000 feet deep. Scientists are still measuring it — and the Greenland ice sheet.

The **Greenland ice sheet** covers all but the outer rim of this largest island in the world. It is over 9,000 feet deep.

Smaller ice sheets — **ice caps** — cover some of the Arctic islands and part of Iceland.

Where the front of ice sheets reach into the sea, they form a floating **ice shelf**. Ice shelves edge two-thirds of the Antarctic continent, but Greenland has only one. That is because most of the Greenland ice sheet does not reach the sea. Its outer edges are too thin to have the pressure needed to move up and over the mountains that border Greenland. So the ice sheet breaks up, like the fingers of a hand. These fingers of ice sheet are **outlet glaciers**. Outlet glaciers, like mountain glaciers, move downward only, through any pass or outlet in the mountains they can find.

As the outlet glaciers squeeze through gaps, they meet up again and join. They grow thicker and larger, and they pick up speed. The largest Greenland outlet glaciers sometimes move at over 100 feet a day. But they don't always move that fast, and sometimes they hardly move at all. Scientists don't know why they slow down or speed up. They hope some day to find out, and are measuring glacier movement with laser beams.

Wherever a glacier ends in water — lake, bay, or ocean — and pieces break off, those pieces are **icebergs**. "Berg"

means "mountain" in the Germanic languages. However, not all bergs are mountainous. There are **bergy bits** and **growlers**, too. Above the water, a bergy bit looks to be about the size of a large house. Growlers are even smaller — about Volkswagen size above the water.

Mountain glaciers produce the least mountainous bergs. These glaciers are narrower and thinner than the outlet glaciers and ice shelves, so the pieces of ice that break off are much smaller. Bergs from mountain glaciers can cause a problem, though. If enough of them break off into a small bay or lake all at once, they can cause a tidal wave.

But truly great mountains of ice are those born from the ice shelves of Antarctica and the outlet glaciers of Greenland.

← Bergs, bergy bits, and a growler on the top left sailing by the coast of Greenland.

3

MOUNTAINS OF ICE

WHEN A COW GIVES BIRTH TO A CALF, IT IS CALLED "calving." Cows calve, whales and dolphins calve, elephants calve — and glaciers calve. Glaciers calve when they break off into icebergs.

How glaciers calve is not completely known. We do know that water, currents, and winds work the floating fronts of glaciers up and down, back and forth, weakening them. Water is also warmer than the ice and causes it to crack and begin to melt. So does the salt in the sea.

Gigantic pieces will usually break off at a crevasse and float away. But smaller bergs calve with a great tumbling and bouncing, crashing down and shooting up high with thundering noises like artillery fire. Finally they find their point of balance and they, too, float off.

These bergs, bergy bits, and growlers melt and crack and calve themselves as they travel. And as their mass changes, they bobble and tumblesault until they find a new

22

Jacobshavn Glacier in Greenland has just calved this huge iceberg, about a mile across, into Baffin Bay fjord.

point of balance. The smaller the berg, the more it tumbles.

Greenland bergs balance and float when 82% of their mass is under water. Antarctic bergs ride a little higher — only about 75% is under water.

So the part of the iceberg that can be seen is very small compared to its unseen underwater section. It's only the "tip of the iceberg" — a phrase that many people use when they mean that only a very small part of something is known or understood.

The large unseen part of an iceberg does not go straight downward, either. It may stretch out far beyond what can be seen above water — and that can be tricky for people

23

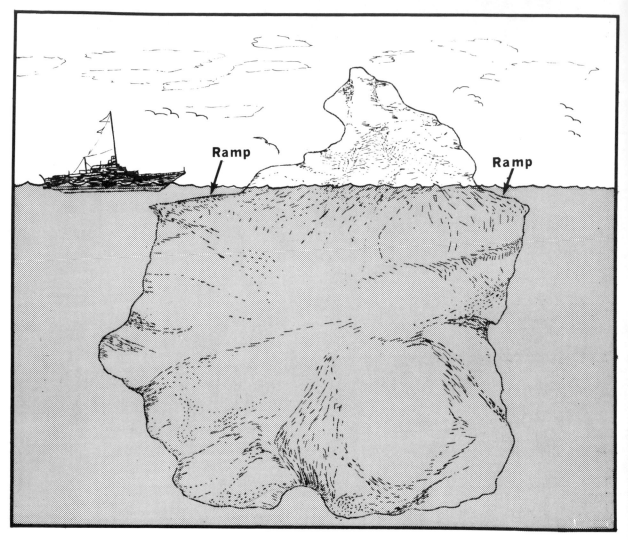

Diagram showing the underwater section of a berg in relation to its tip.

who have to deal with icebergs — or with the "tip of the iceberg."

The shapes of icebergs above and below the water are as varied as the snowflakes from which they came. They may be **domed** or **blocky** bergs. They may be great, flat

tabular bergs. In 1956, a Navy icebreaker in Antarctic waters measured a tabular berg at about 12,500 square miles — only a little smaller than the states of Connecticut and Massachusetts put together. Of course, most tabular bergs are not that big.

This large tabular berg dwarfs the 269-foot *Westwind*, a Coast Guard icebreaker in Iceberg Alley. Tabular bergs are sometimes mistakenly called ice islands. Ice islands are sea ice, not glacial ice. As yet, no one is sure where ice islands come from or how they are formed. Ice islands carry wildlife, and sometimes scientists and research stations.

A berg may have one or more tall peaks or **pinnacles**. The tallest berg ever measured was a pinnacle berg 550 feet high. And that was only the tip of the iceberg!

Icebergs may be smooth or ridged or cracked, or dirty from moraine or bird droppings. (Animals don't live on icebergs, but birds fly over them or perch for a short while.) It all washes off when the berg tumbles. The ocean floor is littered with moraine dropped by bergs as they tumble or melt.

The Coast Guard icebreaker *Eastwind* sails past a 500-foot high pinnacle berg in Iceberg Alley.

A domed berg. The dark lines are moraine or ice-filled crevasses.

The bergs are a heavy, milky white, with light and dark gray angles made by peaks and ridges. They may be striped with thin lines of moraine, or dark green streaks where sea water has entered cracks. Or they may have blue streaks where crevasses have filled with melt water and refrozen. They may carry a pool of blue melt water where the glacial ice has melted, or a pool of blue ice where it has melted and refrozen.

A berg which has just rolled over, or a melting one, loses its solid milkiness and lets some light through. Then the bergs reflect the colors of sunlight, or the blackness of night. Probably the berg that sank the **Titanic** had just rolled and was black in the dark night.

This berg has just rolled over. The dark green stripes come from sea water that has soaked in.

As a berg melts, it sizzles — like soda pop! The sound comes from the release of air bubbles which were trapped hundreds and hundreds of years before, when the glacier was formed.

Their noises, their changing colors, and their movements make icebergs seem almost alive. But they are not. And great danger lies in their uncontrollable movements. Those who understand this stay far away from icebergs. Long ago, seamen sometimes used melt water for drinking — but they risked death if the berg rolled. Today, no one needs fresh water that badly!

It is impossible to tell when a berg will roll in answer to the changes within it, or the actions of wind and waves

28

in a storm. "Any old port in a storm," an old sailors' saying, does not include seeking the shelter of an iceberg! The berg's dangerous underwater ledges and ramps, the suction as it rolls or splits, give no safety in a storm — or in fair weather.

In the last stages of decay, this Antarctic berg may have taken 10 years to reach this melting point. Smaller bergs may take two or three years to melt, depending on size, if they are grounded, and weather conditions.

4

TRACKS IN THE SEA

IN THE OCEANS, ICEBERGS TRAVEL WHERE THE currents and the winds take them. A few Antarctic bergs travel as far north as Buenos Aires, but they do not cross any shipping lanes. In the North Pacific, bergs are small and few. But the Greenland bergs have been a danger to North Atlantic shipping since the voyages of the Vikings. They travel where ships — and people — travel.

Whalers and explorers, looking for the Northwest Passage, had good reason to fear these moving mountains of ice. They could collide with one in a storm or fog, and their small wooden boats would be smashed to bits. If the currents drove them up on an underwater ice ramp, they could be grounded. Or they could capsize if they were too close to a rolling berg. But there weren't many of these adventurous men, and their fates were of little concern to anyone but themselves and their families.

30

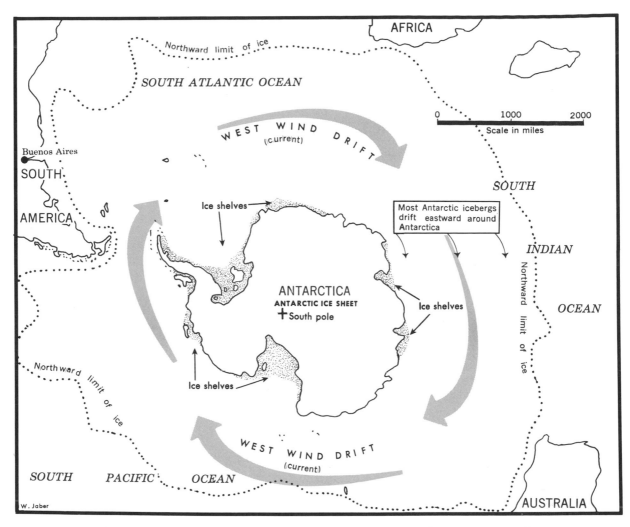

The ice sheet of Antarctica, ice shelves, and the route of the
Antarctic bergs.

Then, in the 1800s, trade boomed between Europe and the United States. Ocean traffic grew tremendously. The great sailing ships were replaced by ships powered by steam. And more and more people traveled across the North Atlantic. Millions of Europeans came to the United States to seek their fortunes, and rich Americans flocked to Europe for its social and cultural life.

The fastest route across the North Atlantic took ships over the Grand Banks off Newfoundland, an important fishing area already crowded with ships. This is also the foggiest area in the world, as the cold air over the Labrador Current mixes with the warm air over the Gulf Stream. There are frequent storms and high seas. And icebergs that have not been beached as they travel Iceberg Alley, move southeast on the Labrador Current, over the Grand Banks.

You can see that something had to be done to keep order in the shipping lanes!

In 1898, concerned countries entered into the North Atlantic Track Agreement, which lasted until 1969. The Agreement set up a highway in the sea, with different lanes, or **tracks**, for east-bound ships and west-bound ones. It solved the traffic problem. It also made it possible for ships to help one another as they followed along the same tracks.

The tracks were set just south of the Grand Banks to avoid the Arctic ice pack, which covers 1,800,000 square miles of ocean. It usually does not move beyond 45° N. latitude, but this changes, and this is the area where ships

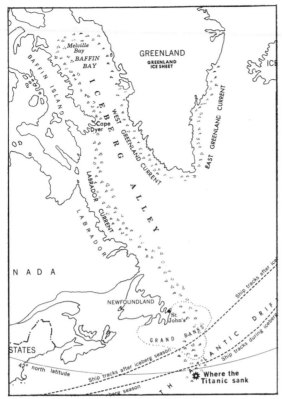

Bergs calving from East Greenland glaciers move south, and sometimes west across the bottom of Greenland. Picked up by the West Greenland current, they join the 10,000 or more bergs calved from west coast glaciers, and travel north up Iceberg Alley. They may spend their first winter frozen in around Melville Bay. Then they swing west and are caught in the Labrador Current, which flows southward down Iceberg Alley. The bergs' second winter may be spent near Cape Dyer on Baffin Island, unless they have been beached, or trapped in bays or inlets, or driven by heavy westerly winds out of the cold center of the Labrador Current into warmer waters to melt.

By this time there may be only a few hundred bergs left to travel the final stage and the last year of the journey—or there may be well over a thousand. These are the icebergs that threaten shipping. Moving south at 10 to 20 miles a day, they finish their journey where the North Atlantic drift of the Gulf Stream mixes with the Labrador Current.

A few hardy bergs have traveled as far south as Bermuda and east of Jacksonville, Florida. They were pretty small by the time they reached there, though. They wouldn't have had the strength to do much more than chip the paint of a ship!

travel. **Pack ice** is frozen sea or salt-water — unlike icebergs, which are fresh-water ice. Thousands of miles of sea freeze in large chunks or **floes.** These floes are held closely together by the action of the wind and the water. Sometimes the force of the wind is so great that the floes pile up against one another, called **rafting** and **hummocking**. Rafting ice looks like two wrestlers standing locked in combat. And hummocked ice looks like one of them has won, and pinned the other down!

In winter, the Arctic ice pack is 10 to 12 feet deep, although rafting makes it very much deeper. In some places the ice pack goes down as much as 65 feet. As the weather starts getting a little warmer, around February, the ice thins a few feet. Some of the ice melts, and passageways called **leads** (pronounced **leeds**) open here and there between the floes. Bergs which have been frozen in the pack ice all winter break loose, and begin grinding their way down leads and through ice to the open sea. Ships trapped in pack ice have sometimes tried to do the same. But leads often go nowhere, ending in ice. And they can freeze up behind a ship, trapping it for months — or forever, if rafting ice crushes its hull.

Seamen know that the only way to avoid the dangers of pack ice is to stay out of it. They are helped by the presence of **ice blink**, a light reflected from the ice pack into the sky. Ice blink is yellowish in clear skies, white in overcast skies, and is seen long before the ice can be seen.

But icebergs do not give off any such warning signal.

A large berg in pack ice. Notice the leads.

No light in the sky, no cold winds, no change in temperature of water or air, no smell, will tell of icebergs in the distance.

Radar isn't much help, either. Radar is far less effective in detecting icebergs than in detecting ships of the same size. And radar can't pick up the low-lying growlers, which are probably the most dangerous bergs of all. They are often impossible to see until a ship is almost on top of them — and they are still large enough under water to slice a ship apart.

How then do ships avoid icebergs?

They keep a sharp lookout, and they listen to the warnings of the people who watch for them — the men of the International Ice Patrol.

5

THE INTERNATIONAL ICE PATROL

THE LOSS OF THE **TITANIC** AND OF SO MANY LIVES, particularly among the well-known, wealthy families aboard, caused great shock and anger. There was a demand for action.

Investigations were held by the United States Senate and the British government. Out of these inquiries came laws for enough lifeboats for everyone on board a ship, for life-saving equipment, and for other safety precautions at sea. And there was strong agreement that a patrol was needed to warn ships of ice along the North Atlantic tracks.

There was no waiting to set up a formal organization to carry out such a patrol. The United States Navy sent two ships out immediately. The next year, 1913, two Revenue Service cutters took on the job.

An International Conference on the Safety of Life at Sea, held in London in 1913, formed the International Ice Patrol, an observation and ice-patrol service. Thirteen

Cartoon published after the sinking of the *Titanic,* protesting the failure of the country to make laws for passengers' safety at sea.

nations agreed to share costs. The United States was asked to run it. The duty was officially given to the Revenue Cutter Service, which became the Coast Guard in 1915. Except for the years of the two World Wars, the Coast Guard has continued the patrol.

Since 1947, the patrol has been carried out by aircraft rather than cutters. A cutter is still used when there are a great number of bergs, as in 1972 and 1973, when there were over a thousand in the shipping lanes. A cutter is also used when the patrol plane is grounded by bad weather.

The positions of bergs and boundaries of pack ice are plotted on a chart. These positions, plus reports of ice that come in from ships and planes in the area, are broadcast twice a day from radio stations in Europe, Great Britain, Canada, and the United States.

Since the patrol cannot keep continuous track of a berg as it moves, a computer at Ice Patrol headquarters is used to give the probable positions of each berg twice daily. It does this by using information on currents and

A berg's record—shape, date and time of sighting, code number.

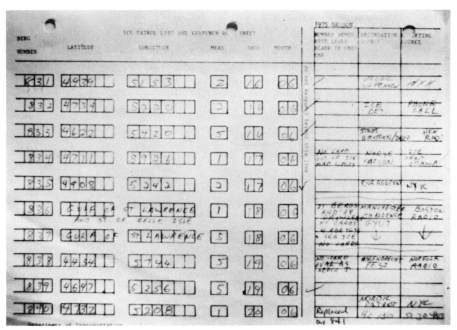

wind direction and speed to predict the drift of the berg, which averages 10 miles a day, but may reach 30 to 40. The bergs are tracked daily on large charts until they can safely be considered melted. The melting point of a berg is determined by the computer and mathematical formulas using time, temperature, and size of the berg.

By gathering all the information they can into the computer, the Ice Patrol hopes that some day they will be better able to predict the movement of icebergs, and to tell exactly when bergs will melt away. They are also working with the Navy and the National Aeronautics and Space Administration (NASA) on improved radar and satellite detection of bergs.

So the safety of thousands of human beings and millions of dollars worth of shipping still depends on one plane patrolling 33,000 square miles of fog-bound ocean. But the men of the Coast Guard have done such an outstanding job that icebergs have not caused a single death in that area during the years they have patrolled.

6

THE MEN WHO TRACK THE ICE

THE INTERNATIONAL ICE PATROL IS HEADQUAR-
tered on Governor's Island, a 7-minute ferry ride from the
crowded southern tip of Manhattan, and across the way
from the Statue of Liberty. The island sits squarely in the
middle of New York Harbor, where the East and Hudson
Rivers meet and flow into the Atlantic Ocean. And not an
iceberg has ever been seen there!

Isn't it a strange place for the Ice Patrol? "Not at all,"
says Commander A. D. Super, Officer-in-Charge, laughing.
"Actually, it's ideal. It's here that we gather in, and give
out, information — and we do that with machines. This is
a large installation and we have all the machines we need
— computer terminals, teletypes, satellite printout terminals.
You can see we don't have to be sitting on top of a berg
for that."

The Ice Patrol plane comes from even farther away —

International Ice Patrol headquarters building on Governor's Island.

the Coast Guard Air Station at Elizabeth City, North Carolina. The plane stops at New York to pick up two or three ice observers, and they fly up to St. John's, Newfoundland. They use the commercial airport there as a base.

The men fly 6 to 8 hours a day, every day that weather permits. When they're not flying, they're checking out the plane. The crew has to do all its own maintenance work. There are no ground crews to do it for them. All of this is hard, tiring work, so the crews change every few weeks of the iceberg season.

It may seem strange, but the iceberg season is in

spring and summer. That's because the bergs are frozen in the ice pack the rest of the time. The ice season may last from February to August if there are a lot of bergs, or from March to June if there are less. In January, the men make one or two pre-season flights up Iceberg Alley to get an idea of how many bergs there are and when to start regular flights.

Each day the plane covers about 1,600 miles of the

The plane's nose moves up so the crew can make repairs.

LCDR Roland H. Buster at the controls of the Ice Patrol plane.

33,000-square mile search area. One of the pilots, Lieutenant Commander Roland H. Buster, explains, "Sometimes we feather the two outboard engines — turn them off in flight — in order to save fuel and stretch the time we can stay up."

Covering the search area properly takes great skill in piloting and navigating. The planes fly down the middle of a 25-mile wide area. One ice observer searches the right 12½ miles, another searches the left 12½. They fly low, at 1,000 to 1,500 feet, sometimes lower, flying under any clouds, fog or mist. They often go down to 400 or 500 feet. Flying at such low altitudes can be dangerous. Parachutes are not much help at that height. Neither are the life jackets.

"A couple of minutes in that icy water and you're a goner — you don't need a life jacket." Scanners Butch Hampton and Edward Allen don't look worried. Scanners are the crew members who, armed with flashlights, keep

MSTC Walter P. Ark watches for icebergs, which he plots on the charts he is holding.

. . . . And back on Governor's Island, MST1 Neil Tibayan charts the information.

Inside the C130 with the ART. Commander Super is on the right.

on the lookout for possible trouble spots in the plane's wiring and hydraulic systems.

When a berg is spotted, its size, shape, and drift direction are recorded. So is the temperature of the water, which is taken from an ART — Airborne Radiating Thermometer. And the navigator plots the exact location of the berg. "It's easy these days. We just ask Igor." Igor is the nickname of the plane's computerized navigation system.

Lieutenants Junior Grade Tom Pigage and John Odom, who take turns as co-pilot and navigator, are enthusiastic about Igor. "In a few seconds he'll tell you where you are and where you need to go. No more dead reckoning. We love him. We treat him well, put him to bed with a pat on the head, feed him. . . ." Tom's voice trails off and he grins.

But smart as Igor is, even it can't keep track of a berg's drift. That is one of the big problems of the Ice Patrol. There is no way of telling for sure where the berg spotted today is going to be tomorrow — or next week.

Radioman Gary McElroy (left) and navigator Tom Pigage with chart keep the plane on its lonely course.

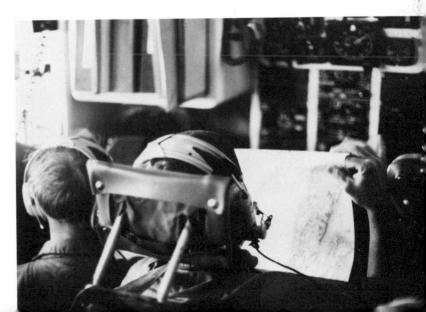

There are little currents within the major currents, surface currents and deep currents. Winds blow at different speeds and affect bergs differently, according to their sizes and shapes. There are physical forces such as friction, the rubbing together of the moving ice and water. These forces are hard to measure, and they all affect the drifting and melting of a berg.

The computer at Governor's Island comes in handy to sort it all out!

"We've tried marking the bergs with dye so we can recognize them when we come back to where we think they should be. But the bergs tumble, and every dye we try washes off, including paint. We set out **drogues** — artificial icebergs made of cork and wood — so we can check drift. We are trying penetrometers, a device attached to a long tether with a signal beacon at the end. It's dropped from a plane and penetrates the iceberg. None of it really works as well as we hoped. Not even the computer. Those bergs just don't always do what the computer says they will!" Lieutenant Junior Grade Thomas J. Neill, also an ice observer, throws up his hands and adds, "There's only one sure way of telling where a berg is, and that's by eyeballing it!"

"But," Commander Super says, "we hope that the over-the-horizon radar that we're testing right now with the Office of Naval Research, or the new Side-Looking Airborne Radar (SLAR) will help. Bad weather won't affect it, and it should be able to tell the difference between a

The computer at Governor's Island.

Dropping a dye bomb—a gallon jar which once held mayonnaise.

whale, a berg, and a ship — which has been one of the problems with radar up to now. So we should be able to keep a radar eye on the bergs. And once we get a satellite up there that will take clear enough pictures through fog and clouds, our whole operation will change. Satellite tracking is not too far off — perhaps three to five years."

"The Patrol can warn ships of ice, but we can't force ships to stay out of it," says Lieutenant Junior Grade Kenneth Knutson, an ice observer. "Sometimes they can't — they have to deliver their cargoes to certain ports. But sometimes they just don't listen. Not long ago a freighter tried a short cut through the ice zone and hit a berg. Luckily no one was hurt, and the ship didn't sink — but the captain had some serious explaining to do."

"We're lucky we only have the Greenland bergs to worry about," Lieutenant Knutson says, frowning. "But the Columbia Glacier at the end of the Alaskan pipeline is showing signs that it might be calving more bergs in a few years. And with all those tourists starting to go by ship to Antarctica, we may have a problem there one of these days — but not soon!" The frown turns to a laugh. "Anyway, by then they may have towed all the bergs away for their water, and there won't be anything left to worry about!"

Towing of the great tabular bergs of Antarctica for their water supply is being seriously considered. Towing icebergs is not a new idea. Between 1890 and 1900, small icebergs calved off Laguna San Rafael in Chile were towed

50

to Valparaiso, Chile, and Callao, Peru, a distance of over 2,000 miles.

Towing a train of four or five huge bergs can be done by atomic-powered tugs. Los Angeles, California, is the city most often mentioned as needing this source of water. The trip would take from one to two years. Even though a lot of the berg would melt, it is believed that there would still be enough water left to make money from the project.

Such a project may be possible and profitable, but it may do more harm than good. No one owns the Antarctic. If one powerful government starts towing bergs, what will other governments do? Will they fight over who takes what? And since the towing would cost so much, no one could afford to give the water away. Will the water have to go to the highest bidder, leaving poor countries to their droughts and starvation? And how will towing affect the animal life of the oceans into which all this fresh water will be melting? And how will taking away huge masses of ice upset the ecology of the Antarctic?

The idea requires much more careful thought and research.

Towing of bergs in the Arctic is already being done, but for a different reason. Rich natural gas deposits have been discovered in Iceberg Alley, and off-shore rigs are drilling there. Sometimes an iceberg moves into the area of a rig. To prevent a collision, company tugs rope the berg like a calf and move it out of the way.

51

Towing an iceberg away from drilling platforms. The towline is the white line from berg to ship at lower left.

But the Ice Patrol can't use towing as a way to prevent ship-berg collisions. They would have to tow thousands of bergs for thousands of miles until they melted!

The Patrol has tried many other ways of getting rid of bergs. They've coated bergs with lamp blacking to make them absorb the sun's rays faster. Nothing much happened. They've planted thermite charges — high heat explosives.

Setting thermite charges on an iceberg. One man, not of this group, was killed while setting a thermite charge.

Before and after lamp blacking. The left half of the berg was blackened. The "after" picture shows only stains and very little change in size or shape of the berg. The danger to the men is great.

This high-explosive bomb scores a direct hit, but does little more than cause a spray of ice.

They've tried bombs. They hardly made a dent in the bergs. Scientists say it would take 1,900 tons of TNT to break up a medium-sized berg. To melt a berg would take 225,000,000 gallons of gasoline!

Since there's no way to keep bergs away from ships, the only thing to do is to keep ships away from bergs. And that is the mission of the International Ice Patrol. The men know how important their work is, because otherwise the tragedy of the **Titanic** might be repeated.

Every year, on the 14th or 15th of April, the men on the Ice Patrol plane pause in their regular duties to toss a memorial wreath onto the waters where the **Titanic** went down. And the daily ice bulletin for April 15th bears the postscript, "**RMS Titanic** 41°46′N-50°14′W. 15 April 1912. Rest in peace."

Tossing the memorial wreath to the *Titanic* from the open rear ramp of the Ice Patrol plane.

GLOSSARY

Bergy bits—small icebergs, between 5 and 50 feet in height above water.

Bridge—the control point of a ship.

Calving—the breaking off of the edge of a glacier in the sea. This is how icebergs are born. Also, the breaking off of a piece of iceberg.

Continental glaciers—ice sheets so big they cover all or most of a continent. Usually used to mean the glaciers of the Ice Ages.

Crevasses—deep cracks in a glacier.

Crow's nest—a partly-enclosed platform for lookouts on a ship, located high above the waterline on a mast.

Drift—earth, rock, and other materials picked up by glaciers.

Drogues—artificial icebergs made of wood and cork.

Firn—last year's snow. Its crystals have a different structure from the crystals of fresh snow.

Fjord—an inlet of the sea, with steep walls. Formed by the scouring of a glacier which later retreated, letting in the sea.

Floes—sheets of sea ice.

Glaciers—Bodies of ice which are formed above the snowline and move because of the pull of gravity and the push of their own pressure. (They are covered by layers of firn and fresh snow, and are kept alive by snowfalls or

58

avalanching snow. Glaciers pick up and carry drift which scrapes the land over which they travel. They drop off this drift, which is now known as moraine, as they move. In this way, glaciers change the appearance of the land.)

Glaciologists—scientists who study glaciers.

Growlers—very small bergs, under 5 feet in height above water, almost awash.

Hummocking—piling up of ice floes by the winds. Not piled as high as in rafting.

Ice blink—light reflected into the sky from pack ice.

Ice cap—small ice sheets. Sometimes used instead of ice sheets.

Ice sheets—the largest glaciers in existence today. There are two, one covering Antarctica, the other most of Greenland.

Ice shelf—the front of an ice sheet, floating on the sea but still connected to land.

Iceberg—a piece of glacier that breaks off in the water and floats away.

Iceberg Alley—the waters between Greenland on the east and Labrador on the west, through which the Greenland bergs travel.

Laser—a pencil-thin, powerful beam of light. Even the tiniest movement in a glacier will change the beam of a laser shining on it. This change is then measured on a special machine.

Leads—open water between floes of pack ice.

Maiden voyage—first voyage of a ship.

Moraine—earth materials dropped by a glacier.

Mountain glaciers—glaciers that start on a high mountain top, usually in a basin called a cirque (serk) glacier, and move downward through valleys, where they are sometimes called valley glaciers.

Outlet glaciers—the thinner outer edges of ice sheets that break up and move downward through any passes or outlets they can find.

Pack ice—ocean ice, sometimes called field ice. It stretches out in great fields or packs in far northern and southern latitudes. Pack ice does not usually go below 42°N.

Penetrometer—a device used experimentally to track icebergs.

Piedmont glaciers—glaciers formed by mountain glaciers which end on a flat plain and spread out.

Plateau—flat area of land

Radar—an instrument that uses radio signals to locate objects. The signals bounce off objects and return like echoes. These echoes are recorded and plotted to give locations and movements.

Rafting—The piling up of ice floes caused by the action of winds. Higher than hummocking.

Snowline—the altitude above which there is always snow on the ground.

Starboard—on ships, the right side.

Stern—rear of a ship.

INDEX

M

melt water, 18, 27
moraine, 16, 18, 27
mountain glaciers, 16, 19, 21

N

National Aeronautics and Space
    Administration (NASA), 40
natural gas, 51
Navy, United States, 37, 40
Neill, LTJG Thomas J., 50
Newfoundland, 8 (map), 32, 42
New York, 9, 10, 41, 42
North Atlantic Ocean, 8 (map), 9,
    14, 30, 32, 41
North Atlantic Track Agreement,
    32
North Pole, 18
Northwest Passage, 30

O

ocean, 19, 30, 32. *See also* North
    Atlantic Ocean; Pacific Ocean
Odom, LTJG John, 47
Office of Naval Research, 50
off-shore drilling rigs, 51-53
outlet glaciers, 19, 21

P

Pacific Ocean, 30
pack ice, 32-34, 39
penetrometers, 48
piedmont glaciers, 18
Pigage, LTJG Thomas, 47
Plymouth Rock, 16
Pole Station, 19

R

radar, 36, 50. *See also* Side-looking
    Airborne Radar
rafting, 34
Revenue Service, 37-38. *See also*
    Coast Guard, United States
Rockies, the, 16

S

St. John's (Newfoundland), 42
satellites, 40, 41, 50
scanners, 45
scientists, 10. *See also* glaciologists
Senate, United States, 37
shipping, 30-34, 38, 40
ships, 9, 11, 12, 28-32, 34, 36, 37,
    39, 44, 50, 55
Side-Looking Airborne Radar
    (SLAR), 48-50

Smith, Captain, 9, 11
snowfields, 16
snowline, 15
South Pole, 18
Statue of Liberty, 40
Super, CDR A. D., 41, 48-50

T

thermite, 53
Titanic, the, 9-13, 27, 37, 55-56
tracks, 8 (map), 32, 37

U

United States, 32, 37, 38, 39, 40

V

Valparaiso (Chile), 51
Vikings, 30

W

whalers, 30
winds, 22, 40, 48